A FIRST LOOK AT HORSES

By Millicent E. Selsam and Joyce Hunt

ILLUSTRATED BY HARRIETT SPRINGER

WALKER AND COMPANY N

Library of Congress Cataloging in Publication Data

Selsam, Millicent Ellis, 1912 —
   A first look at horses.

   (A First look at series)
   Summary: Lists various kinds of horses and
explains how to tell them apart.
   1. Horses — Juvenile literature. (1. Horses)
I. Hunt, Joyce. II. Springer, Harriett, ill.
III. Title. IV. Series: Selsam, Millicent Ellis,
1912-   . First look at series.
SF302.S44   636.1   81-50735
ISBN 0-8027-6429-0   AACR2
ISBN 0-8027-6430-4 (lib. bdg.)

First published in the United States of America
in 1981 by the Walker Publishing Company, Inc.

Published simultaneously in Canada by Thomas Allen & Son
           Canada, Limited, Markham, Ontario

Trade ISBN: 0-8027-6429-0
Reinf. ISBN: 0-8027-6430-4

Library of Congress Catalog Card Number: 81-50735

Printed in the United States of America

10 9 8 7 6 5 4 3 2

A *FIRST LOOK AT* SERIES

For Jennifer Knopp

The authors wish to thank Lieutenant Richard Risoli,
Troop F, New York City Mounted Police,
for his help with the text of this book.

This baby horse is called a *foal.*
It is nursing on its mother's milk.
All mammals feed their babies with milk.

Horses belong to a group of mammals
whose legs end in hoofs.
Hoofs are horny coverings that protect the toes.
The horse has just one hoofed toe
at the end of each of its four legs.

There are names for the different parts of horses.

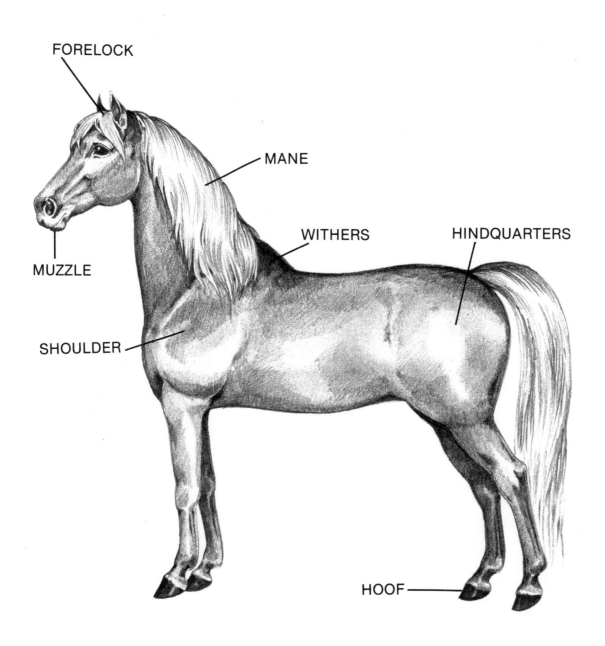

FORELOCK

MANE

WITHERS

HINDQUARTERS

MUZZLE

SHOULDER

HOOF

People measure the height of a horse
by putting their hands next to one another
from the ground to the top of a horse's withers.
Each hand is about four inches wide.
How many hands high is this horse?

All horses were once wild. People captured them, tamed them and used them to do different jobs.
Now we have three main kinds of horses.
You can tell them apart by their size.

Heavy horses have large bones and thick legs.
They can weigh twice as much as light horses
—about 2,000 pounds (900 kilograms).
These horses are usually about 16 hands high.

Light horses have smaller bones and thinner legs.
They weigh about 1,000 pounds (450 kilograms)
and are usually about 15 hands high.

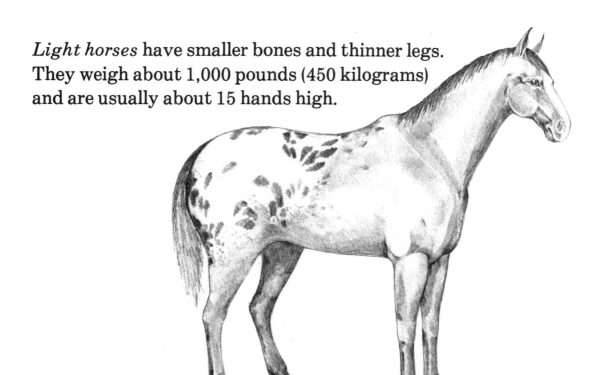

Ponies are the smallest horses.
Any horse that is less than 14.2 hands is a pony.
A pony weighs about 500 pounds (230 kilograms).

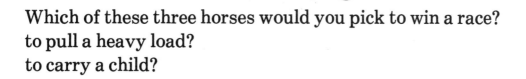

Which of these three horses would you pick to win a race?
to pull a heavy load?
to carry a child?

PONIES

How can you tell one kind of pony from another?
Sometimes size is a clue.
The Falabella is the smallest pony.
It is only seven hands high.

The Highland pony is the largest pony.
It is usually 14.2 hands high.

Sometimes the hair is a clue.
Find the pony with a lot of hair on its feet.
Find the pony with a long shaggy tail, mane and forelock.

SHETLAND

DALE

HEAVY HORSES

The heavy horses are called *draft horses*.
They were once used to carry knights in heavy armor.

In many parts of the world these horses
are still used to pull big loads.

Most draft horses have a lot of hair on their feet.
The Shire has long white hair on its feet.

The Shire is the tallest horse
in the world.

The Belgian has long dark hair on its feet.

The Belgian is one of the strongest horses
in the world.

The Percheron has very little hair on its feet.

The Percheron is often
used in circuses.

LIGHT HORSES

The Arabian may be the first horse ever tamed by people.
It is gentle, fast, strong and hardy.
For these reasons it has been bred
to many other kinds of horses.

Look at the Arabian's head.
It narrows down toward the mouth.
It is so narrow that people say
it can drink from a teacup.

Look closely and you can see
a curve just below
its large eyes.

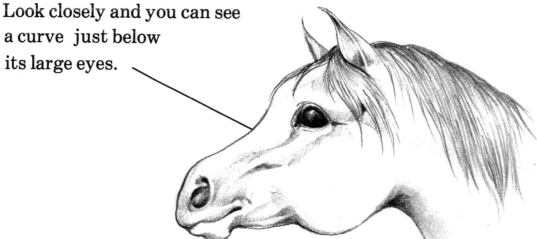

Look at its plump cheeks.

Both the Thoroughbred and the Quarter horse
are light horses used for racing.
The Thoroughbred is the fastest horse in the world.
Notice its long neck, long body and long thin legs.
From its nose to its tail it looks like speed.
The Thoroughbred can race long distances.

This horse is also fast. It is called a Quarter horse because it usually races a quarter of a mile. You can always tell this horse by the powerful muscles in its hindquarters.

The Quarter horse is one of the horses cowboys ride.

These two light horses are not race horses
but they are comfortable to ride.
They both carry their heads high.
The Saddlehorse is graceful and tall.
The Morgan is chunky and small.
Which is which?

These three horses can be told apart by their markings.
Find the horse with small spots.
Find the all-white horse.
Find the horse with dark and light patches.

LIPPIZANER

22

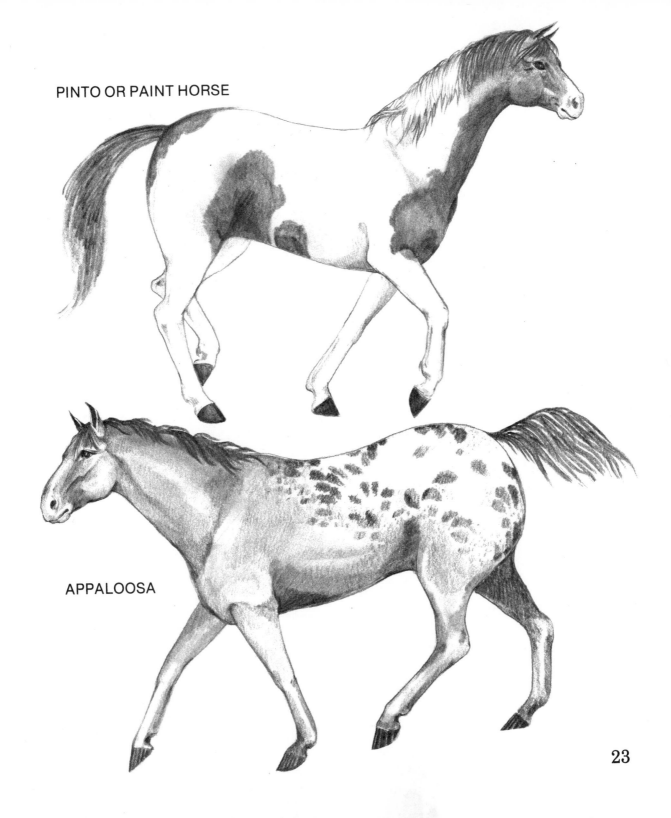

PINTO OR PAINT HORSE

APPALOOSA

23

There are names for the white markings on a horse's head.

BLAZE

STRIPE

SNIP

STAR

The leg markings also have names.

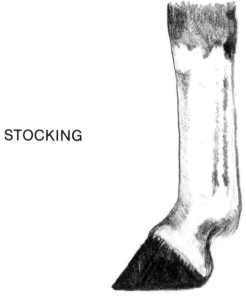

STOCKING

SOCK

The Przewalski (shi-VAL-skee) is the only
really wild horse left in the world.
It has a head like a donkey and a short thick
mane that stands straight up.
There is a black streak along its back
and the lower parts of its legs are black.

Are these horses?
These animals are relatives of horses.
The zebra has many stripes.

The wild ass has a stripe down its back
and sometimes another stripe across its shoulder.
It also has very large ears.
When a wild ass is tamed, it is called a donkey.

To tell different kinds of horses apart:

Look at the size.

Look at the hair on the feet.

Look at the head.

Look at the hindquarters.

Look at the markings.

WORDS TO REMEMBER

Draft horse—a heavy horse.

Foal—a baby horse.

Forelock—the hair that hangs over the face of a horse.

Hands—a measure—the width of a hand—used in measuring horses.

Hindquarters—the rear end of a horse.

Hoof—the horny covering of a horse's toe.

Mammal—an animal that nurses its young with milk.

Mane—the hair on the back of horse's neck.

Withers—the highest part of a horse's back.